Bring Your Own Bags

bag for good

Use this bag again and again. If it gets damaged, we'll replace it for free.

No More Waste

This is a **cotton bag**.
We can put fruit
in this bag.

This is a string bag.
We can put vegetables
in this bag.

This is a paper bag.
We can put bread
in this bag.

This is a paper bag.
We can put mushrooms
in this bag.

Look at this bag.

We can put ice cream

in this bag.

This is a **hessian bag.**

We can put our shopping in this bag.

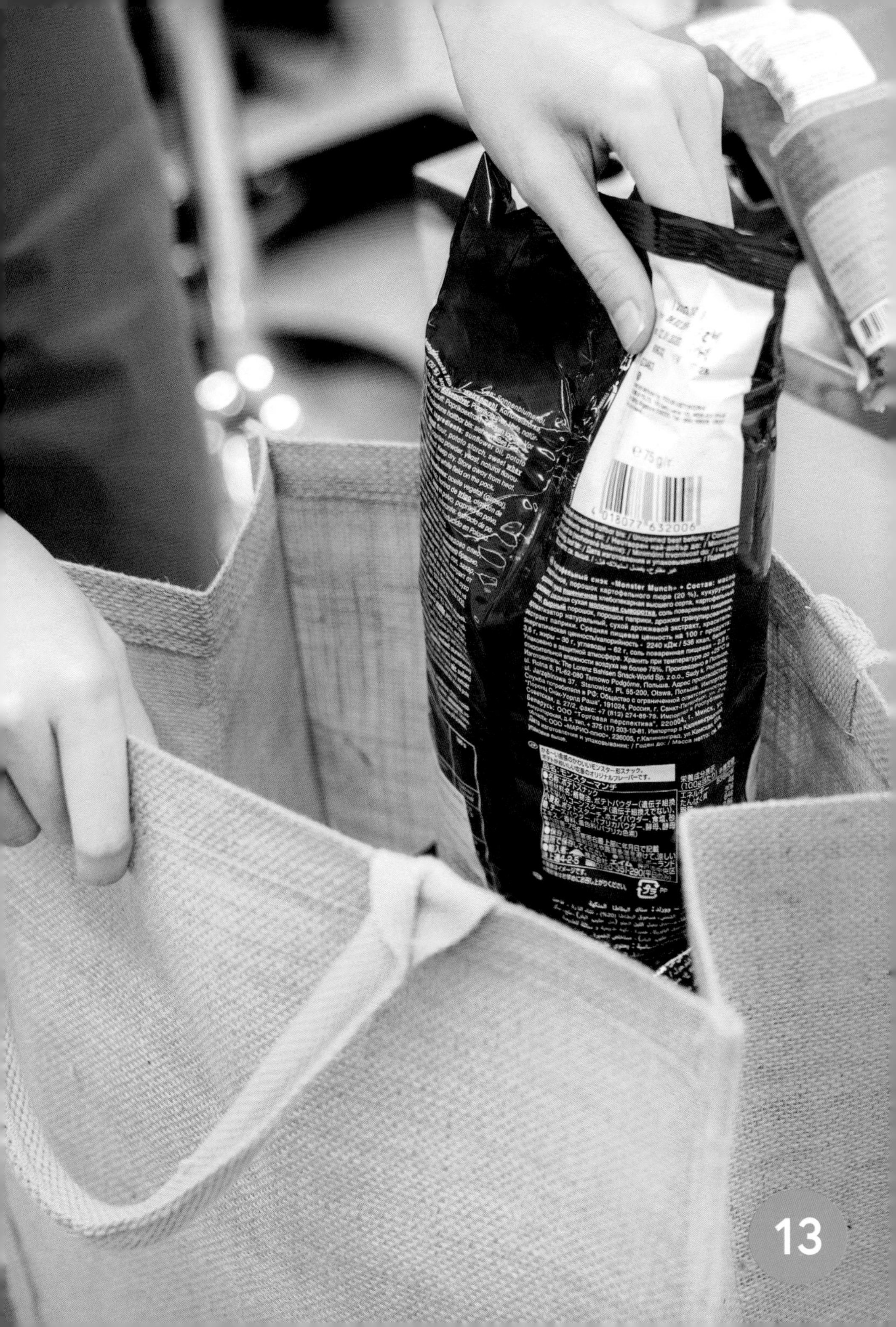
«Monster Munch»
75g/r
4 018077 632006

Look at our shopping.

15

cotton bag

hessian bag